DIVINA is DIVINA

DIVINA
is
DIVINA

Jack Wiler

CavanKerry ◊ Press LTD.

CavanKerry Press Ltd.
Fort Lee, New Jersey
www.cavankerrypress.org

Library of Congress Cataloging-in-Publication Data

Wiler, Jack, 1951-2009.
Divina is Divina : poems / by Jack Wiler. – 1st ed.
p. cm.
ISBN-13: 978-1-933880-20-4 (alk. paper)
ISBN-10: 1-933880-20-1 (alk. paper)
I. Title.

PS3573.I4286D58 2010
811'.54–dc22

2010000026

Cover art Robert Piersanti © 2010
Cover and interior design by Gregory Smith

First Edition 2010, Printed in the United States of America

NOTABLE VOICES
CavanKerry Press

CavanKerry Press is proud to publish the works
of established poets of merit and distinction.

CavanKerry Press is grateful for the support it
receives from the New Jersey State Council on the Arts.

For my beloved, Johanna

A Note from the Publisher

Regrettably, shortly after *Divina Is Divina* was accepted by CavanKerry Press, Jack Wiler passed away. Since he is not here to speak for himself, I, as publisher, have the privilege of speaking for him.

The process of creating a book involves an intimate blend of efforts among the publisher, writer and editors. With Jack's passing, his literary legacy was now in the hands of his writer friends. Scores of people came forward to tend to Jack's work and to make sure that the finishing touches to the book did not in any way suffer from his absence. I can think of no more perfect example of the grace of community working than the book that you hold in your hands.

Central to the process at every stage were Jack's good friends Teresa Carson, Danny Shot and John 'Mack" McDermott who copyedited the book, chose additional poems, wrote cover and flap copy and bio, chose selections for cover art, secured permission for an author photo, and helped the publisher and graphic artist finalize the overall design. Painter Robert Piersanti generously donated the cover art as did Laszlo Bardos the author's photo which was taken at Jack's last reading. Baron Wormser, a steadfast believer in the importance of Jack's legacy to literature, edited the book and wrote an introduction elaborating on that legacy. Alicia Ostriker and Bob Holman read the book and offered to write blurbs. Poems from the book have been read at various tributes and memorials to Jack, and two of those poems

A Note from the Publisher

"Dreaming of Imps" and "My Friend Asks Me to Write About Losing Things" were published in the latest issue of the *Journal of NJ Poets*.

And so, the community that Jack so respected and loved has brought *Divina* into the world. Heartfelt thanks to all of you. Jack's memory and his work are blessed for your exquisite care. All of this advance tribute to *Divina* and Jack's poetic gifts, we believe, will go a long way to bring *Divina* to its readers and will keep Jack alive through his poems among us. And so it should be. He was a mountain of a man and poet; his poems will outlive all of us.

—Joan Cusack Handler
June 2010

Contents

Contents

Coda

Introduction

This is a posthumous work. Jack Wiler died in October, 2009. When a poet dies, one faces the uncanny terrain of verbs—the poetry, at once, is and was. It exists here on the page to be taken up by the living but there won't be any more poetry written by the hand that wrote it. One feels this crux strongly in the case of Jack Wiler because this book testifies to how powerful and increasingly complex Jack's writing was becoming. There are poems in this book that can stand beside any poems in this era.

Anyone acquainted with Jack's poetry knows that Jack always was writing powerful poems. However, as he got older, and as he went through the travails of AIDS which brought him near death, he changed. Jack did not become a spiritual poet in any conventional sense. Jack had no conventional sense. He wasn't interested in that. He did, however, forge his way into territory that showed he had thought deeply about the terms of mortality. This was not to put a sad face on anything. On the contrary, Jack's poetry became even more celebratory about the sheer incredible fact of being alive, a fact that surely is the basis of all poetry. At the same time, Jack was not one to make anything out to be any better than it was. He knew the wages that were extracted and he recognized those wages in poem after poem.

As a poem from this volume such as "We Monsters" makes plain, Jack worked as an exterminator. For many people this work is one of those occupations that is necessary but would never be spoken about. Jack did speak, however. He found himself both in his vocation and in his fight for life in a place that few writers ever enter, a place where all the careful bets about what should be are irrelevant. This place where no-mercy and mercy came together gave Jack a special perspective on the sheer brutality of existence—lives are crushed without a second thought—and the determined grace of all creatures as they seek to live their lives. In this regard, Jack had the remarkable gift of being able to see both sides at once. Sometimes this could feel like sheer perversity but it ran much deeper than that. It enabled Jack to step outside of himself and into the lives of other people and creatures and moments. It enabled him to annul time, another basic function of poetry.

Someone who does this may be called among other things a shaman, someone who does the vision work that the society needs in order to exist as anything like a coherent society. Jack didn't seek this role nor did he avow it. He routinely mocked the paraphernalia of vision. That seems understandable since poetry is perennially an underground movement in the United States. We never know where our bards are going to come from or how we should honor them as bards. I do know that Jack's poems are stirring in the way one wants poetry to be stirring—utterly alive to the human comedy in all its pathos and modest glory. They exist in the perennial present tense of poetry. They are the inestimable gift he left to the living.

—Baron Wormser
April 2010

Ay, in the very temple of Delight
Veil'd Melancholy has her sovran shrine,
Though seen of none save him whose strenuous tongue
Can burst Joy's grape against his palate fine:

John Keats;
"Ode to Melancholy"

We Monsters

At work every day for weeks I've been drowning.
People pestering me for answers to questions that have
answers they don't want.

Yes, you have mice.
Yes, you have cockroaches.
Yes, you live in a nice apartment.
Yes, your apartment has a high rent
and you are an important person.
Yes, you are smart.
Yes and yes and yes again.

But, no.
Think about this for a minute.
You live in New York.
The sewers are lined with roaches.
The Chinese restaurants swarm with roaches.
The rats come out each night from burrows by the parks
and feed on your leavings.
Drink from the last drips of your iced coffee.
Nibble at your spilled salad.
Slide insistent into your restaurant's basement and
scurry happy through a world of food.
Not unlike you.

You're the only living thing that should be happy here?
Flies haven't the right to light on your cast off soda?
Fungus gnats shouldn't graze happy on your drain?
Cockroaches shouldn't congregate in the dark spaces in your
        cabinets?

You're their landlord.
You're their parents.
You are their God.
Why not be happy with that?
Why not stroke their hard skin, their rough fur?
Why not offer them some wire for gnawing, some toy?
Like you do your dog.
Your cat.

They have no right to these things?
No right to joy?
Jammed up thousands at a time in the tiny spaces behind
your cupboard?
Forced to forage on your leavings like wretches?
You, the rich landowner, throwing them scraps and bits and still
you begrudge them even that
and call me to bring their lives to a close
because you pay so much in rent.
You tyrants.
You monsters.
Filled with privilege and power unable to spend one minute with
them and their stupid little lives.

There may be some parable here.
Perhaps you are the cockroach.
Perhaps you are the rat.
Perhaps one day you will scurry out from the subway platform
onto the train and sing a song begging for food.
Perhaps you will turn away.
Perhaps you will say, I have no time for this.

All of us huddled in this mess.
Hunting for food.

Sipping at tiny draughts.
Taking brief respites.
All of us rats and mice and roaches and ants.
All of us monsters.

Big Mouth

Jaws flapping all the day.
Yakkety yakkety yak.
Talking and talking and talking
and just when you think
I'm all talked out I find something
new to talk and talk and talk about.
None of it matters; no one listens.
It's like talk radio Wiler 103.6.
All talk all the time.
Angry Jack.
Funny Jack.
Jack in high dudgeon about
injustice or the proper use
of the pluperfect subjunctive.
And I know it all.
I know who wrote *Strange Fruit*;
who was Spain's most popular
bullfighter.
I know so much that
I have to tell you.
Smart boy in the first row,
hand up, begging for attention.
Teacher's pet.
Encyclopedia Jack.
Annoying jerk that can't sit still.
Not even for a second, not even
to watch the stars careening
cross the sky.
Jack the jibbering monkey;
running round and round
the room, naming everything.

4

Never once looking at the room.
Its shape, its mystery,
its dumb silence.
Always ready with an answer.

My Friend Asks Me to Write About Losing Things

I ask her, what kind of things?
Keys?
Change?
I misplaced my passport once.
Is that what you mean?

She says no.
Things that mean something to you.
I say, like my car?
Like my tv?
Like my favorite chair?

She says no.
Things anchored in your heart.
Like a lover.
Or a job.
Or a house.
Or a place.

Those kind of things.
I say, oh, that should be easy.
I've lost all of them.
It was easy.
I grew ill.
I came close to death and all of it went away.

She says no.
The things you have now.
I say, all I have now is two dogs.
A car.
A new car.

I have a nice garden with a gazebo.
I have a few friends.
I have a lover.

She says maybe those are the things but maybe
you're not good at this.
I say, no, I'm good at losing things.
I've lost clothes and skis and bikes.
I've lost golf clubs and baseball gloves and shoes,
a nice pair of slip-ons I bought in Miami.
I've lost books and records.
My ex-wife has six hundred of my records.
I've lost suits and socks and money and houses.

She says, what about the lover?
I say, oh.
I say, oh.
I say, that's not so easy.
That's something that can't go.
That's like part of my body.
My heart.
My blood.
She says, the doctor took your spleen.
I say, oh.
She says, every day for a few hours you lose the sun.
She says, every day for a few hours you lose the moon.
She says, if you weren't so smart you'd know the lover is the moon.
You'd know the lover is the sun.
You'd know losing your lover is like losing your life.

I say, yes, but I almost lost that.
She says, almost.
I say, ok.

I say, so what should I say and she says you're the poet.
You figure it out.
Talk about dying.
Talk about waking up one day in a house filled with only one person.
Talk about losing your heart.

I say, oh.
I say, oh, oh, oh.
I say, I don't want to lose anything.
I say, I want my six hundred records back.
I want my skis.
I want my golf clubs.
I want my apartment.
I want my rosebushes.
I want everything back.
I say, I don't want to lose anything again, ever.

She says, Oh.

Mourning Doves

I walk my dogs each morning at six.
The youngest gets things done quickly.
The older dog takes her time.

At the end of the first block I hear
the call of a mourning dove.
If I'm lucky I hear the answering call.

All my life I've waited for the answering call.
Every day at 6:15 I hear the request.
Some mornings I get the answer.

Love Poem at the Beginning of Summer

This is a love poem about empty places.
About blank walls.
About light in the night and noises on the street.
This is a love poem where no one is there.

This is a love poem for you.
This is your house.
This is the light you make.
The soft light of a summer night.

The noises from the bar down the block.
The girls screaming at their lovers.
Your clothes spread across the bed.
You spread across the bed.

The sun in the afternoon.
Too hot sometimes to bear.
The smell of your skin.
You mixed carrots and soda for tanning cream.
That taste is this poem.

This is a poem without you in it.
Like every love poem should be.
A poem with an empty heart.
A poem with a smell you can't quite name.

I say you smell almost like cotton candy.
You show me your perfume and it's cotton candy.
I say you smell like my life.
You show me getting up and going to work and coming home tired.

I say I love you and you say I love you
and we could say that over and over and over.
But all I know is the spray of tanning oil on the deck.
The spilled Corona.
The taste of your breath, thick with beer and tobacco.

This is a poem with no one in the house but me and two dogs.
This is a poem with the deep sighs of my dogs.
The breeze from a summer night.
The wail of a siren.
The music from my neighbor's radio.
Cumbia.
Soft mountain music.
Music about places and islands I've never seen.

Your hair is scattered on the sink.
Clothes are tossed on the bed.
The dogs are snoring.
The girls and boys from the bar are yelling.
It's a loud poem. It's a poem that won't let me forget.

So I wander out and look at the pale Hudson County sky.
I can't see a single star.
The moon is hazy with neglect.
The dryer is turning and turning.
The dogs are tossing.

Everything in the world is asking about you.

My Mother Says Happy Birthday

I don't think of my mother very often.
She's been dead for a long time.
Last night I dreamt she sent me emails.
Wishing me a happy birthday.

Happy birthday.
From a dead woman.
From a frail woman who never wore nice clothes.
Who walked to work in the library twice a week
wearing a cloth coat and a practical cap.
From a woman who sat in her corner of the couch
each evening reading a novel.
Or the newspaper.

Who made me iced tea on a summer evening.
Boiled the water, soaked the tea bags in the water,
added the sugar.
Then let it sit.

A happy birthday from a dead woman.
How do you take that?
A bad dream perhaps.
A bit of bad meat,
as Mr. Scrooge famously said.

She had short brown hair.
When she was young she aspired to be a painter.
Her father let her go to the Philadelphia College of the Arts.
But no further.
Young women were to have children.

And what kind of children?
Children that ran wild in the backyard.
Children that yelled and rampaged and caroused.
Children that were alive with life.

I am her child.
I write these poems.
Every day, I write them as though she could read them.
It's not sad.
It's just the truth.
She never saw a single word of my writing unless it was an essay
from my school.

I have no children.
They have no dreams.
They never read my words.
When I was getting better from my illness in 2002 I went to the
    library
where she worked.
In the basement were all of the books from my family's library.

What is a library?
What is a crypt?
What should you do with a mother that is long dead?
When she left she was young.
You could say my brothers and I made her life a misery.
You could say my brothers and I made her life a joy.
You could ask these questions until they toss the soil
over your grave.
The answer would be the same.

I would like to answer those emails.
I would say, I write poetry.

I would say, I care about words and the way they make the world.
I would say, if I could, I would make you and yours dance again
on the stage.
Poor Mrs. Wiler.
I can't.
I can only dream.

On Death and Dying

I'm in a house with five people, all infected with HIV.
One or the other of us could die, either sooner or later.
Two days ago my lover's father died.
Not suddenly and not unexpectedly.
He was an older man with health problems and
she knew it was coming.

We all of us here in this house know it is coming.
It's still a surprise.
This one leaves happy and drunk and three days later
is in St. Vincent's never to come back.
That one hacks and coughs and drives you nuts but
nothing seems to set her back.
I drag myself to work and watch tv and golf and
drink wine and cry and forget most of the time
that the hand of God is brushing up against me.

Remember warm January days
when you think it will never snow?
Remember the slow trudge through sleet and stiff wind
just weeks later?
Remember cool days in June
when you think it will never be hot?
Remember lying in bed dripping in sweat thinking
oh, when will it be winter?
Remember being so sick you saw angels at your bedside?

They haven't left.
It always snows.
Ice covers the roads and cars crash suddenly and
a man stumbles out and grabs his chest.

It's always too hot, the humidity so great it seems like
your breath is steam like you'll never be cool again.
Death is always there.
She takes your father, your friend, the man at the 7-Eleven.
Sometimes you're sad, sometimes you forget to pay attention.
Then someone is rattling the end of the bed.
A candle burns thick black smoke.
Tears and sorrow fill the air.
You try to raise your head but can't.

Hoboken in June

I go to Pier A and
lie in the sun,
a skinny old white man
in a sea of young people
all tan & fit.
One group is even tossing
a football & across the way
they're rebuilding the
rotting ferry slips.
The girls & boys are
beautiful but I get hot & thirsty
& walk down Washington
to look for beer & food
which I find
& while I'm drinking
they close Washington &
the Hoboken Puerto Rican Heritage Parade goes marching
by with the mayor & some old
Puerto Rican guy & the mayor's
chief rival looking embarrassed somehow & then comes
Miss Puerto Rico
giant tiara & gown
surrounded by a dozen little
Miss Puerto Ricos.
All waving to me
all saying hello
waving like Jackie Kennedy
on a hot day in Hoboken
on the first weekend in June.

Futbol and Gowns

We spent two hours arguing about the capitals of the
countries of South America and I had to bring out my atlas which
was ten years out of date and even though neither of us
spoke the same language we argued.

She watched the news with a passion that amazed me.
She was arguing about everything and nothing and I understood
nothing she said. She could have had Marxist ideologies or
socialist or monarchist. I don't know.
But she was passionate.

She wore dresses and bras and had the worst hair style
on the planet and she loved futbol.
Did I mention she was a man?
She begged for shit without
begging and drove me nuts.
She was contrary and arbitrary
and all without a word I could control.

She was a friend from another planet.
She sang to my dogs.
She sang.
She was short and argumentative
and wouldn't try to learn English.
She drove me crazy.
She shuffled around my house and coughed
and drove me crazy.

She sang to my dogs.
She sang.
She sang to me.

The song she sang to me was sad.
It was a song of loss.
It was the song of a sailor far from his home,
washed up in a foreign land.
He longs for his home but he can never return.
It was a song of joy.
The song of a sailor who left his home because
his father disowned him; who can never return.
The song of a sailor who has found some friends
but they can neither understand the other.

Today I walked outside and heard the song of the mourning dove.
That was her song.
Persistent.
Repeating.
The song that comforts us.
The song that tells us we have this place for just a few hours.

From dawn till dusk.
From birth till death.
From friend to friend.

Vaya con dios mi amiga.
Mi alma es tu alma.
Para siempre.
The world is filled with tears and the song of birds.
Para siempre.

Divina Is Divina

My beloved had a friend.
My beloved is Johanna.
Her friend is Divina.
Of course, my beloved's real name is Marko
and her friend's real name is Hector.

My beloved brought Divina to my home.
She spoke no English.
I spoke no Spanish.
Of course I spoke a little Spanish and
Divina tried a little English.

My beloved and I have two dogs.
Divina loved our dogs and took them out.
When she came to visit she would stand outside
and cry, Johanna, and inside the dogs would cry.

My beloved's friend Divina died.
Not suddenly. Not prettily, not like anyone should die.
She died in a hospital in the city of New York
and no one knew her name.

She was Hector Gomez.
She had no family.
She lay quiet and still and faded into the world.
No one in the hospital knew Divina.

If we had stood outside and shouted her name
they would have walked us to the side
and asked us to leave.

They wouldn't have been jumping up with joy to hear our cry
like my dogs, like Johanna, like me.

So my beloved's friend met her end alone.
In a city hospital.
With no dogs prancing around her.
No flowers blooming.
Even though it was spring.

You could say, and you should,
what the fuck is this?
You could be angry, and you should.
What kind of world tosses humans in the trash?

But that would be like asking why the leaves
blow in the fall.
It would be like asking why flowers wilt in hot sun.
It would be like asking why Hector is Divina.

Hector is Divina because the flowers bloom!
Hector is Divina because the sun rises!
Hector is Divina because she is.
Because we are.
Because the sun is.
Because we die.
Because.
Because.
Hector is Divina because we need to hear
someone outside our door crying our names.
Divina is Divina.

Surgical Options

My doctor has suggested I need a splenectomy.
My platelet count sucks every time I go on Interferon treatment
and he thinks if we remove my spleen I'll be able to tolerate the
drugs and thus,
thus,
avoid certain death from liver failure.

I'm a smart guy so I researched splenectomies.
It turns out the spleen is attached to your heart.
It turns out that the surgeon might,
might,
pierce your heart
and the whatever, lower ventricle or aorta or something
will fill your abdominal cavity with blood and
well,
you could die.

When I tell my friends about this they're mad at me for
minimizing the risks.
I tell them I'm not.
But I am.
I know that given my godawful luck the incompetent
nincompoop I hire to remove my spleen will rend
my heart in two and I will bleed to death in minutes.
All this work gone in two heartbeats.
I'm not even sure if heartbeats is one word or two.
But by the time I will have figured it out I'll be dead.

I've been taking nasty medication for six years.
I shit in my pants at work.

My dick doesn't work right when I want it to.
People look at me like I'm some sad sack
cancer patient and now I have to deal with dying right away.

I was fairly prepared for death in twelve years.
Well, actually, twenty.
But right away while I'm asleep that seems wrong.
And to remove something that's not even fucked up.
That seems really, really wrong.

I'm not really interested in dying just yet.
I'm especially not interested in dying because someone makes a bad
        move.
Like a bad putt from two feet out.
Or topping the ball on the tee.
Anyone could do that.
I watched Tiger Woods blow a two footer for birdie just last week.
So I'm a candidate for death because some poor fool has a bad day.

That seems wrong.
Ok, dying from AIDS is okay.
That's my fault.
Dying from Hep C.
My fault.
Dying from sniffing too much blow.
My fault.
But dying because some guy blows a two foot putt with nothing on
        the line.
Wrong.
It's as though someone said, listen,
We've arranged a speaking tour for you,
it's the most important tour of your life,
you'll be a star.

The opening event will be a press release at Windows on the World on September 11th at 9:00 a.m.

Oh Jesus.

Spring Peepers

My friend Bob writes to me about spring peepers.
Frogs that make a lot of noise in the spring.
It's a mating thing.
In South Jersey where we were young the frogs were everywhere
and their peeping filled the spring night.
I can remember coming home after a spring thunderstorm to find
frogs everywhere.
Dropped by a storm.

There aren't any spring peepers in Jersey City.
There are a lot of small birds and there are two mourning doves.
There are a few flowering trees and a dozen or so daffodils
on a two block stretch.
On the first beautiful day of spring I lay in the sun
drinking cold Corona with lime and salt.
I went downstairs to Caribbean Nights and shot eight ball
with Franklin, Louisa's boyfriend.
I came back and cooked ribs.
Seven stars shone in the sky.

When I was sick the sound of peepers and crickets filled the air in
        Wenonah.
My ears were thick with their buzzing and peeping.
The air was fragrant with spring flowers.
You could lie drowsy in the spring day without a care.

Cares I had then and cares I have now.
The sweet smell of spring is a blessed gift.
The noise is still there ringing in my ears.
Far away I can hear an approaching thunderstorm.
There is a brief flash of light.
The taste of beer and salt is sweet on my lips.

Praises for the Insect and Mammalian Dead

I had a nice day today.
No one cursed me.
It was cold today.
Not as cold as yesterday but
I have the feeling it will be colder tomorrow.

It will be cold, thank God, for several more months.
Men will stumble up to me on 9th Avenue and ask for money.
They will say it is for food.
Perhaps it is.
My friend Jane's boyfriend died suddenly from liver disease.
This should not have been a shock but it was.
To her.
To his children.
People will call me to solve difficult problems involving
mice and rats and other pests.
They will be arrogant and they will be willing
but they will be desperate.

They will be asking me for answers that aren't simple.
I will fail in my explanations.
I will offer biological and social explanations but in their fear,
in their worry, they will dismiss them.
To the people that I talk to everything I say is stupid.

Like everything we say to a lover we think is leaving.
Don't go.
Don't I do this or don't I do that.
Didn't I buy you this or didn't I comfort you then.

It's all stupid.
My consolation and explanations are all hollow.

Real.
But hollow.
You have mice.
You have them because you're a human in a densely populated
        region
of the world populated by a rich mess of other humans.
Not everyone gives a shit about mice like you do.
Not everyone lies awake worrying about the bedbugs biting.
Some of them come from places where the bedbugs are like flies.
Some of them come from places where if you raise up your head
someone else will lop it off.

Cherish your mice, your rats, your roaches, your bedbugs!
Love them as you love your sons and daughters.
They are your children!
They live with you as much as you with them.
They huddle in little clutches terrified of destruction and they don't
        even
know about terrorists or nuclear devastation or satellites.
The little bugs and mice are the meek.
They wait patient under your stove for your castoff crumbs.
For your drops of water.
For the condensate on your pipes.
They are your poorest children.
They have no other home but yours.
You wretched misers of capital.
You own your apartments!
You own your lawns!
You own your skin and your hair and your sons and daughters!
You have lovers like me and you wish you owned them too but you
        don't.
You hold them close on a winter's night and know they can leave.
Like a breeze or a laugh.

But all of you muddle under the same dull January sky.
Each of you struggles for a bit of food, a spot of conversation,
the day your boss says, oh, what a nice idea.
The day your lover says, I love you too, and
the day you wonder if she does or if you do.

This is the time to consider what will come.
Spring and rebirth and a thousand mice and cockroaches.
Ants and termites and love.
You'll strut down the avenue and duck into little cafes
and they'll feed off your leavings happy as pets.
You and your lover or your family will talk and laugh and drop
    crumbs
as carelessly as lies or compliments.
They are your children.

They will grow strong and happy and democratic.
They will feed at the common table.
They will join with the bacteria and the viruses and the multitude of
    plagues
to usher us into the world of paradise.
Say all power and all praises to our children!
Grant them health and joy!

All Things Come to Him Who Waits

I'm sitting on the couch with my dogs
who are barking, barking, barking.
Loud, heedless.
Loud. Insistent.
I pay no attention.
I've just returned from the ER
where I sat for hours at the side of my beloved.
She was in pain at times, comfortable at others.
The threat of death sat just outside the door.

Another dog.
One without a name.
One both of us know and
one both of us would prefer not to have in the home.
He is neither regal nor elegant.
He is not insistent.
He is patient.
Just as the doctors and nurses ask us to be: patient.
Just as we are: patients.

In the background of any hospital is the horrible buzz of noise.
Beeps and screams and bumps and shouts.
The banter of nurses, the orders of coffee,
the yawns of the housekeepers, the doctors asking, who is this?
Who is this?
The rooms filled with sick and well and all of us
must listen to the insistent high whine of people who may
or may not be dying.

Maybe they are just vomiting.
Maybe it's just the flu.

Maybe they are lunatics coming in from the cold.
Maybe they can't speak the language.
Who can?
At my side is my lover.
Quiet.
Fever consumes her.
The rush of bacteria and its compelling urge to finish its business
is everywhere in her body, in her world, in my world.
The bacteria cannot hear the yelping in the background.
The beep, beep, beep of the machines.
The angry cries, the stifled moans, the curses laid down by the ill, the
      dying,
the stupid, the people that they inhabit.
The bacteria are home.
Eating their quiet meals with their dogs about them.
Happy, contented.
It is a rich day in their short lives.
Some of them raise a glass of celebration.
Others worry about tomorrow.
Will there be food?
Will there be solace?

So there we all are in the waiting room of the ER in Christ Hospital.
The room named for the savior of the human race.
We are shitting in our pants.
We are moaning about our legs.
We are asking again and again, where is the doctor.
We are complaining about the complaining patients.
They are not patient.
We are tired.
All of us.
Even we bacteria are tired.
We've been eating and breeding and sleeping for what seems like
      years

and still we die and our homes are destroyed and our future is
    always uncertain.

We are all of us dogs.
Waiting for the master to bring us food.
Waiting to go out.
Patient.
Patients.
Our just reward will come.
Poisons and wishes.
All things to think about as we kneel at the foot of the bed
to say our little prayers.

Why I Like Money

I like money because I like food.
It's true you can make your own food
but using money makes it easier.
I can grow vegetables.
Not many though,
my space is small.
I like beef.
But the space question makes
that impossible so I'm left
with a small pig or chickens.
Chickens would work best but
if you want anything other than eggs
you have to kill them.
Then you have to pull off their feathers.
I think I've read you have to hang them upside down
for a period of time to allow the blood
to drain from their bodies.
I have no idea what you do with old chicken blood.
Next you have to pull out their guts.
Finally, after months of waiting for them to grow
up and hours of struggle getting them ready to cook
you can toss them in the oven.

Or, if you have money, you can go to the store.
There, in aisle after aisle is food.
Lots and lots of food.
Chickens with their guts conveniently removed.
Pieces of cows and pigs.
Bottles of milk.
Eggs by the dozen stacked all nice and neat.
All you have to do is wheel up your cart

filled completely with food to the register
and give them money.
That's why I like money.

I like money because this poem isn't worth money.
That's the other reason I love money.
There's no money in poetry unless you put it there.
I like poems about money.
I like to hear paeans of praise to the all mighty dollar.
The rants of poor paper pushers against the monied.
The cruel jokes of miserable little fools complaining about the rich.
They're poor and they wish they weren't.
That's the nice thing about poetry.
You can tear up bags of money and throw them in the trash
and no one ever cares.
In real life if I see a dollar bill on the street I count myself lucky.
In my other life I can ridicule the fools who work for money.
As if I don't.
As if money grew on trees.
As if chickens came packed in little boxes stacked in some store
for any poor fool to buy, to pop in some oven and eat.
As if anyone would believe that.

Talking With Nat

Today I spent the end of the day talking with Nat.
Nat is a tall, black man in his sixties.
He worked as a printer for most of his life.
Before he became a printer he was a drug addict,
a stick up man, a con man, a crook.
He was, in his own words, a disappointment to his mother.

Nat and I talked about regret.
About what we could have been.
Both of us working at Acme Exterminating.
Me a salesman, him a part time stock boy.
A stock boy.
A man that used to stroll into "policy joints" with a shotgun
cocked and ready.
We each regret the stupid choices we made.

He remembers his wife.
He thinks of the house he could have had.
He talks of children unborn.
Of money pissed away.
Not so different than me.

I tell him it's not that bad.
I say, wasn't it a gas to knock over a joint?
Wasn't there a rush of pleasure to run down the
street with a sack of cash?
He says, Yeah man.

He says, but I could have had a nice home.
I could have gone into the army and they'd have made a man of me.
I say, but you are a man.

He says, I could have moved back with my wife.
We could have had children.

I say, me too.
We all could have done things a little different.
But for a bad pick here and there we all might
be accountants in nice houses in Lakewood.

But there's something to be said for sitting in a little room
with your friends.
Smoking good weed and planning some wild scheme.
Then getting up half cocked and doing it.
Then when it's all over you're sitting alone in a room with a bag of
        money
laughing and laughing and laughing.

It's probably wrong to take huge amounts of drugs and make
everyone you love think you're a worthless piece of shit.
But they never get to sit in that room.
And you do.
God gave me and Nat a gift.
He gave me AIDS and he gave Nat a job as a printer.
He said pay attention and we did.
But he took away something too.
We'd really rather be running down the street
whooping like wild Indians with the joy
of our preposterous dream.

Yes, we're just going to get high with the cash.
Yes, it's just somebody sucking your cock.
Yes, it all blows away and you get old and die.
But the gift we got wouldn't mean as much
if we didn't understand the price.

So me and Nat are sitting in Acme Exterminating
on a lovely August afternoon talking about what
could have been.

Explaining My Life

I don't have any money
even though I work
and collect disability.
I don't have nice furniture
or a nice car but that's
not too bad.
You might say, well at least
you have your health,
but it wouldn't be true.
I don't have my health.
I pretend I have my health
so people won't feel
obligated but inside I
know I'm broken.
Broke and broken
and old and alone and tired,
asleep most nights by ten.
I'm not sad though.
I have a dog and a lover
and I can see birds
leaping up from the cross
on the spire of St. Ann's
and I get to eat anything
I want.
It's priceless really and
I paid dearly for it.

Advertising in the Dark

The other day I thought I saw
a commercial for a Hummer.
This was between 14th & 23rd
or maybe between 14th & 9th
but it doesn't matter
because it's impossible.
We're in a tunnel.
The windows open on walls
that haven't ever seen light.
I think it means I'm nuts.
Crazy as a bedbug.
Driven mad by this stupid job,
my loony boss,
the hunt for a new apartment
in a city where a parking spot
is 500 a month
I must be crazy.
Why else would I look
out the window in a
tunnel?

How to Succeed in Pest Control

It's important to know why you've
taken a position in the industry.
Is it for money?
Is it for career advancement?
Have you always been fascinated
by the lives and habits of insects?
Are you concerned about social
issues? Protecting property or
saving people from disease?

Perhaps the answer is not quite so clear, perhaps it's a business
your wife inherited or
that you purchased with
your savings after losing
a job you loved.
Perhaps you just took the job
because you needed a little
money. You were young and
it looked like an OK job.
Ride around all day and spray some shit out of a can, maybe
bang some housewife on the side.

Only now you're married with two
kids and a wife and it's not enough
anymore so now you want more.
Now you want success,
or prestige, maybe run for
Congress, maybe open a couple
branch offices but the whole
thing eludes you so you come
to me and I've got twenty

years in the business, a magazine column,
a cute blonde wife and that must mean something and it does.
It means I'm a failure,
just like you.

Succeed in pest control?
You poor fool.
Success in pest control
isn't measured in money
or prestige.
It's measured in bodies.
It's measured in the long
journey to a deep
basement.
It's measured in blood,
in broken bones, the snapped vertebrae of rodents.
You can make all the money
in the world but
if you don't slap
at every fly that passes
you've failed.
Every time a cockroach
climbs out of a heating
duct at two a.m. while
you're on the can is just
one more reminder of
how little you've achieved.
Success in pest control
is success in the darkest
places of your heart.
Impulses long suppressed
now eagerly embraced.

To succeed something
must die and you
must be the instrument of
its death.

Things I *Can* Say In East Brunswick HS

I can say extricate.
Or fractious,
or I could say fricative.
I could use culpable, unctuous, even lugubrious.
I could talk about the battle of Verdun and how
three hundred thousand men and boys
perished under the withering fire
of machine guns in just a few
hours.
Withering.
I could use that word.
I could talk about the soup
of blood & mud & chunks of flesh.
The dead men & boys who
should have been home
baking or farming or arguing
about Cicero.
Or I could talk about the
men swaddled in Kevlar
trundling through the streets
of Baghdad in a dented Bradley.
They would let me say that,
let me describe the sudden thud
of the improvised explosive device.
The shocked faces staring
at the legless man sitting
across from them.
Their faces spattered in blood
& shards of bone.
In minutes the femoral artery drains.
I could say

sweet Jesus
but that would be all.
This mess needs a good
Anglo-Saxon curse
a coarse rebuff to
fools & death.
Rough consonants of anger.
But no.
Only a muttered phrase.
The averted gaze.
The lost opportunity for anger.

My Beloved City

In the weeks before I became ill
New York was attacked by two airplanes
filled with unwilling passengers.
The airplanes struck the World Trade Center and thousands
were killed in a matter of an hour.
Some leaped to their death, others were incinerated,
vaporized was the word the newspapers used.
For weeks and months after the event
I read their names and small stories.

That was nearly five years ago.
The dead are dust.
Some are still found on rooftops of nearby buildings.
You'd think this would be sad.
You'd think it would make you sob deep gasping sobs
and you would be right but you would be wrong.
You should get up and walk a couple blocks north or
wander up to where I work on 9th Avenue and watch
the real world pass by.

Stop at Soul Fixins and eat some fried chicken and drink some
        lemonade,
stop at the Twins Bar and drink a long draught of ale.
Walk a little further and step into the Market Café.
Order a glass of wine and some olives and cheese.
Say hello to Robin who's been there since the 90s.
Ask him how his kid is doing.
Ask him about the neighborhood.
When you're done with your wine go to Esposito's and
order some sausage or pork or steak.
Listen to the flood of customers.

The banter in Spanish and Italian and English.
People asking for pork bellies and prime cuts and
how the fuck do you even think about cooking a pork belly.
Go further and stop at the Bellevue Bar and have a glass of Bud,
then up to Rudy's for another and a free hotdog.
Say hello to the hookers and the gimps and the methadone addicts
walking up and down the street
arguing about their benefits.
This is our city, our argument, our beer, our food, our dead.
If it's raining get wet.
If it's cold and there is damp snow kick it and think
soon it will be spring.
If it's spring throw your head back and roar and know
soon it will be so humid you can't breathe and
the subways will devour you with their heat.
So good.
Go downtown.
Go to the Bowery.
There are hardly any bums anymore
but if there are some throw them a buck and
then stop at the Bowery Poetry Club.
Listen to bad poetry, good poetry, stupid poetry,
dull poetry, odd poetry, NY poetry, academic poetry.
Think.
Where else in the world can you have all this in one day
and then go to the Bowery Bar and eat a good meal.
Maybe meander down to Loisaida.
The Nuyorican.
Gathering of the Tribes.
Say hey to Steve Cannon and his harem of young girls and listen
to the best writing in New York.
Get on the L.
Go to Brooklyn.

God knows why but my friend Danny says Brooklyn is fun.
Me, I hate Brooklyn.
It's Hoboken about to happen.
Go to Queens.
Go to Jackson Heights, eat churri churri, eat Brazilian, drink
    caipirinhas,
eat feijoida, eat pupusas and red beans and rice and tacos
and drink Modelo and then find an Irish pub
and sip a long slow Guinness.
This is New York.
German and Irish and Salvadoran and Puerto Rican.
It's Brazilian and Polish and Italian and English and stupid white
    trash.
It's soul food and Harlem and Striver's Row.
It's three thousand dead people that got killed by nine or so idiots
    from some nation that thinks we're crusaders.
The dead numbered dishwashers and secretaries and accountants
and actuaries and traders and ad people and cops and firemen and
none of them gave a fuck about the Middle East
but some dipshit decided they had to die
but what they couldn't kill was the city.
The Nigerians and Ghanians and Cubans and Bolivians and
Egyptians and Saudis and Israelis and stupid chumps from Iowa
all come here for one reason.
This is the city of choice and change and roil and rush and mess and
disaster and money and chance.
You come here to change.
The men who drove those planes changed.
From flesh to ash.
The people in the buildings changed.
From flesh to ash.
Everybody else got on the train the next day and went to work
and said, fuck this shit, we've got money to make, we've got bills to
    pay,

we've got women to fuck, we've got clothes to make, we've got food
to cook, we've got food to eat, we've got to put on a show.
And tonight, somewhere in some stupid little theater in some place in
NY
five or six people are putting on a play.
They have ten or twenty friends in the audience.
If they're lucky their friends will gasp in delight or laugh in
amazement.
If they're not they'll nod their heads and say, nice show.
But they can't do it in Nebraska.
They'd be arrested in Chechnya.
They'd be shot in China.
They'd be beheaded in the UAE.
They can be who they are and eat what they want and fuck
who they please and fuck everybody that drives a plane into that
and fuck everybody that tries to fuck with that with force of arms
because what gives it power isn't force of arms.
So, lift a glass of ouzo with me.
Dosvidanja.
Salud.
Cheers.
God Save the Queen.
Fuck y'all.
And drink it down and drink it deep,
it's the drink of New York.

Prometheus

The girl across from me is beautiful.
It's February and it's cold.
The train lurches around a curve
in fits and starts
and I realize I'll be doing
the same thing tomorrow
and tomorrow.
The girl will always look away.
My train will pull in right on
time, like it can't wait to
take me to hell.
The waters of the Hudson
look bad, like the sewers
of New York have disgorged
their foul bile all at once.
O joy, where are you?
O happiness, beauty, why have
you left me chained to this
terrible fate?
Prometheus bound!
No!
Prometheus lost in the spiral to death?
No Prometheus shrunken,
shriveled.
Reduced to writing contracts &
managing insignificant databases.
Prometheus, deskbound.
Prometheus riding the 4 train
back and forth,
to and fro.

O woe!
O horrible patience.
Give me rest or money.
Give me spring.

Let the girl at least glance
back one time on this
terrible ride.

Siberia

The train is not going to
Manhattan.
I'm not going to work.
The train is a re-education train
and we're off to the Gulag.
The train is filled with artists & poets & poor souls
turned in by their children.
Just last week they had good jobs in some ministry,
finance or postal,
now they lurch in unison
as we head towards Vladivostok
& starvation & moral
salvation & illumination
but for now we are just waiting.
All of us riders in the dark
of the steppes in late spring.
Cold one day.
Hot the next.
Always hungry.

Love, Death, and Detective Work

We found the body about two hundred feet up the ravine.
It was covered in a pair of jeans.
They were damp with urine.
The head of the man was nearly detached
from the neck,
but not quite.
There were flies filling themselves on the dried blood.
On the way up, we walked over crushed glass,
till we came to a drawer full of crystal.
Mikasa, Waterford.
All glistening and all broken.
Some of it red with new blood.

She was some fifty feet further up.
Wearing denim shorts and a t-shirt and sobbing.
She was shaking.
Her feet were torn and crusted with glass.
You could see the bloody footprints
all the way up the ravine.
The buzz of flies filled the air.

She said,
I found him like this.
She said,
He wanted to talk.
She said,
He wanted to tell me something.
Then he went out.
Who could have done this?

Her hands were wet with blood and sweet with its smell.
She might have cradled his head but not likely.

She was sobbing but there were no tears.
She said, he wanted to tell me he'd found someone else.
Someone else.
Someone else.
Look at me.
Why would you want someone else?
She brushed a fly from her forehead.

I turned away and walked back down the ravine.
We all leave our spouses, in one way or another.
She was a little more abrupt.
The buzz of flies fills my head more days than I'd like.
I can remember my second wife
calling my phone, leaving long, rambling messages.
You could hear her taking drags off her cigarette.
She'd say, you're a dick.
She'd say, you should die.
Neither of us did.
But she did throw the Waterford at me with great force
and I loved that snifter.
She did take my records and my books and she gave
my skis to some dick in the neighborhood.
One winter day I watched him zip by, all tall and clean.
I didn't piss my pants.
She didn't slit my throat.
I didn't toss her in the bay.
She didn't cut off my dick.
But we betrayed each other in ways that were unimaginable
just two years before.
Oh, to be in love,
to hold your loved one's head in your hands
and caress his head and give him a dainty kiss.
I've longed for that too much, too often.

The Nature of Desire

It's midnight and an old girlfriend calls to ask me my favorite sex
scene. She's looking for a new boyfriend on-line and she's answering
the standard on-line questions that are designed to find the man or
woman that's right for you and I give her my first answer which is
Jimmy Stewart and Donna Reed kissing in *It's a Wonderful Life* while
Sam (Hee Haw) Wainwright is on the phone from New York City and
in kissing they're admitting that they need each other, that they want
each other, that once they have each other there's no New York City
there's only stupid dull fucking Bedford Falls and for the first time in
Jimmy Stewart's career, but not the last, he's hot and it's all because
he's about to fall, but then I think of other favorite sex scenes and
I have to add talking to Willa my dispatcher yesterday afternoon
about getting hammered by the cops and while we're talking I can't
help but notice her ample bodice, her tits, really, and her wide and
welcoming grin and the tough stance she takes with the NYPD and
that leads me to Jessica yelling at me about Caroline and she looks
real good and then I think about Johanna on the counter of her
friend's kitchen and kissing her long and deep and then that brings
me to Patty in the attic of my parents' house, my room and it's 1970
and it's hot and we spend hours going over the geography of each
other's bodies and we start by just bumping up against each other
and that reminds me of one afternoon several years later in a dorm in
New Brunswick and for some reason I can't remember, Patty and her
future husband Alan are there and we're talking about sex and Alan
says something about how you can't just give somebody an orgasm
and I beg to differ and I say I can prove it and I say I can prove it
with Patty and we go to my room and prove it again and again and
again and again and maybe that's my favorite sex scene but that
would rule out being with Tammy in 1981 and we're staring at each
other across a bar and we can't even talk to each other but we love
to fuck but that would rule out my ex-wife Mary who made so much

noise we both would laugh and that would rule out my first time with Peter with a shaved head and that would rule out Johanna and her huge cock and that would rule out the rough feel of skin on skin and lip on lip and the heave of bodies and the stupid laugh and the odd cries and all the things that make every time you do it your favorite sex scene in a movie.

The Poet Confronts Popular Invention

My niece called in sick from school today while I was visiting.
I was the responsible adult and had to determine if she was ill
and if she should stay home or report to school and
I said, she is ill.
She should stay home.
I said to her, take an aspirin, get a lot of rest and try to get better.
She's 17.
Barely a girl, barely a woman.
She's smart and sexy and a disaster waiting to happen.

Later in the day, around 3, her boyfriend came over
to see how she was and because she appears to be
responsible and because I appear to be not suspicious
I let him in and he goes back to her room and for the next half hour
I make excuses to visit the hall outside her room but at last
I become sleepy.
It's a beautiful day in spring
filled with pollen and magic and flowers and
I've been drinking beer and lolling in the sun and
now I fall asleep on the couch listening to Jack Benny
in *The Horn Blows at Midnight* and suddenly in my sleep
I'm awakened by my niece's cry.
In my sleep it sounds just like the noise all my women make when
        they come.

I wake up.
You would too.
Then I hear her laughing and then a few minutes later,
really, not that many,
she comes out fully dressed and happy.
What am I to think?

You know what I mean.
Did she come?
Was she being tickled?
Am I a stupid befuddled uncle asleep on a couch on a spring day?
A man, dipped in fairy dust,
asleep, his senses dulled, his judgment beclouded
by the girl, the day, the flowers.
Maybe everyone.

That night I watch a movie.
Finding Neverland.
It's about J.M. Barrie.
The British playwright who wrote *Peter Pan* and in fact
it's about how he wrote it or really about how some
guy figured out how he wrote it and it wrenches my
heart because while I watch I'm next to my nephew Doug
who's rubbing the neck of my dog,
who's spent the past three days running like a child through
the woods with my dog.
Who for all intents and purposes might as well be a dog.
Who talked with me that night about how to be a man
and in his innocence and ignorance my knowledge seemed ugly.
He believes that by acting a certain way or by looking a certain way
girls will like him.
Like him.
As if that has anything to do with the way men and women get
      along.
As if that has anything to do with passion and cum and tongues on
      rough beards
and pubic hair and the hard thrust of cock into pussy and the
      satisfying
grunt of joy and then the way a man can make a woman cry out
      again and again.

It really has nothing to do with who likes who or who is more polite
    or dresses
right or has a good haircut, it's just the pull of man to woman and
    we really
have very little control of that.
But he wants to know why I want him to cut his hair
and all I can think about is him running down a trail with my dog
    Cookie.
Both of them stupid and young and heedless.
And that takes me back to this movie
where they show you first J.M. Barrie tying a kite string to a kite,
then the kite in a play,
then the play performed before the children who flew the kite
and I think this poem is like that.

My nephew is a child for just a brief moment more.
My niece is a woman but not quite.
I am more than aware I will die.

I could reach here to make this poem more important than it should
    be,
but what you should take from the poem is this:
When at the end of the day I peeked in my niece's room
she and her boyfriend were asleep.
All their clothes were on.
They looked like children.
They wanted to be adults.
They had the power to make me shiver with terror at what might
    happen to them.
Their brief cries were like loud alarums.
They will grow up probably break up meet others have children and
    die.
This is the sweetest moment of their life.

The Love Poem Johanna Asks For

She asks for a love poem.
She says it has to be done in a week.
I say, sure.
I say, I can do it easy.

Then I go to sleep and dream.
I dream all the things people dream and then
I get up and work and work and people intrude.
I work and I come home and I eat and my love poem
fades and fades.

She doesn't.
She is here every day.
Large and happy some days.
Small and scared on others.
The music loud, the beer cold, friends all around,
but really it's only she and I here.

She and I and the dogs we picked.
They run through the house like my love.
On the porch are our flowers.
It's fall now so some of them are collapsing from
a rich summer of sun.
Like sometimes Johanna and I collapse after a day at the beach.

Tired and drunk.
Happy and laughing.
Ribs on the grill, friends all around arguing over this and that.
But always on the porch all I can see is Johanna.
She fills my house.
She makes our house.

She strolls through the rooms trailing smoke and joy.
She screams bloody murder at the dogs.
She lolls at her leisure and calls me at work to say,
I'm lonely.
Me too.
I'm lonely.

All around me people are yelling and angry.
Trucks are stuck in traffic and
my coffee gets cold but I can see her on the porch
with the dogs jumping like maniacs
happy like me to come home to her.

This is our house.
The house we made.
A house we prayed for and received.

We have a porch and flowers and an office
and a bedroom and a living room and a kitchen.
Johanna works hard doing what she doesn't want to do.
I work hard doing what I have to do.
But all the time I see her on the porch,
twirling around in the sun.
Laughing and laughing.
Spinning joy out of nothing.

So.
She asks for a love poem.
She gave me lots of rules.
She says I should talk about how we live a life most people don't.
We do.
She says I should talk about how she feels.
I don't.

Divina Is Divina

Because all I can see is her on the porch,
dancing with our dogs,
smoke billowing around her,
flowers blazing in the beautiful sun.

Sometimes you get exactly what you want.

Milo in Jersey City

I was in a box.
They took me out of the box to piss and shit
and they put food and water in the box.
Around me were dozens of other dogs.
All in boxes.

Then the two came.
They took me out of one box and put me in another.
That box moved.
Then we came to another place
that was dozens of large boxes
and some of them were outside.
There was food and water on the floor everywhere.

You could call this heaven.

Food on the floors.
Water on the floors.
Boxes that open into other boxes, that open out into the world.
I go out with the mother they gave me and we keep everyone
else from our boxes.
We bark and bark and bark.
It's so wonderful to make so much noise.
Small birds and bugs and other things come to our boxes and I chase
        them.

No, this is heaven.

This is heaven.

Boxes and food and water and bugs and dogs and barking.

A New Prayer

Spider beetles.
Clover mites.
Confused flour beetles.
Carpenter ants.
White flies.
Fungus gnats.
The myriad of creatures
we notice at our worst moments.
Strung out on coke we
see a drain fly and scratch
till our arms bleed.
We enter menopause
the children leave home
and we become convinced
paper mites (an illusory pest)
are biting our ankles
and in our anguish
we howl to all of our
discomfort and
they see us as we are,
bereft of strength and
courage.
Weak in the sure
knowledge of our death.
But we don't see the
microscopic struggles
of the insect.
Its own efforts to secure life.
No.
We slap and scratch
and drown it in noxious poisons.

Pity us oh lord in our blindness.
Do not cast us away
like the shed skin of some
cockroach.
We do not leave our father's home.
We sometimes forget the
way
and
the place.
But we know it is home
and for that we beg forgiveness.

My Fucked Up Heart

It's beating too hard, or else too fast.
It gets broken, like an egg,
too often.
Sometimes I feel like I'm
making omelets every day,
breaking all these eggs,
breaking this bruised muscle.

How did it come to this?
It was fine.
Except for the one time all the
blood drained out my wrist
it's never faltered.
Two marriages, cheating girls,
lying friends, messy affairs, all
that shit and it held up fine.
All of a sudden it becomes
fragile when I'm happy.
When shit works, it doesn't.
Wretched chunk of meat!
It betrays my courage,
sits me down on my bony ass
and quits.

What am I to do?
I can't just get another,
like a pet or a girl or a hooker.
I'm stuck with it,
stuck with its crumbling
chambers and encrusted arteries.
Stuck with its foolish whims

and false bravado.
Forced to limp home
each day thinking that
today will be the day
it gives up the ghost
and leaves me a crumpled
heap of old rags
lying on the sidewalks
of New York,
people stepping gingerly
around this sad, ruined pile.

What You Can Do in Central New Jersey at Christmas

I go with my friend Bill Wasnak to Sayreville or Jamesburg,
one of those central Jersey towns with one long street,
low, one and two story buildings and a half dozen dozing bars.
We walk into one and there are all my friends from twenty years ago.
Big Mike, Debbie Fried, Alan Estevez, Bob Zirpoli, Jack Ward,
the Irregulars, all standing around, happy, drinking, laughing.

I'm talking to Pete Keen and I ask him where he's living now.
He says the North Carolina coast.
I say, what a coincidence, I go there often.
I ask Bill, didn't we go there, what, two years ago?
He laughs, takes a drink, and says, no.
The last time we were all there was the fall of 2001.

The fall of 2001.
What a cruel joke.
Now I understand.
Now I see the bar for what it is.
The ghosts of Christmas have washed me up just short of Christmas
        Day
in a dingy old man's bar with all my lost and forgotten friends.
Bob Zirpoli, who hasn't spoken to me since 1981.
Pete Keen, Christ, for all I know he's dead.
Wasnak, married now, with two boys and a lovely wife.
Prosperous businessman, avid golfer, man on the go.

I look around again and see the glasses covered in dust,
the windows boarded up.
Waiting for the wrecking ball from some developer's dream.
The Melody Bar crushed by the jaws of some great earth-moving
        machine.

The Court Tavern huddled up against the New Brunswick of
    tomorrow.
My friends old and fat and drinking too much.
Working at jobs they hate.
Making too much money, or too little, with wives they abhor or who
    detest them.

O horrible dream. O stunted joy.
O Melody Bar.
A band now long forgotten plays some creaking punk anthem.
The smell of stale beer and lost love stinks up the joint
and we reel out into the dawn
asking, where's the party, where's the party?
Once someone would have said,
I am the party.
Once, we would have laughed and laughed.
Now we stare at the harsh dawn sun, turn our separate ways,
march back home.

It's hours till Christmas and the ghosts have not found me fit for
    redemption.
They offer this happy gathering, my long forgotten friends,
this bar, this grim lesson.
O Christmas.
O Joy.

The Angel of Death

I watch lots of movies with angels in them.
I'm always amazed that they look like the angels I knew.

I understand the purpose of angels.

The purpose of angels is to help us deal with another life.
We don't know what the fuck they're talking about.
We have sex.
We eat.
We sleep.
It may surprise you but all of these things carry mortal consequences.
Mosquitoes bite you in the night.
You get syphilis or gonorrhea or AIDS.
You get dysentery, you get cholera, you get typhus.
You die.

But most of the time here there is only this.
Living.
You can say, thank you. You can say, have a nice day.
Then you can pick up your cell or your phone.
You can get in your car.
You can hug your wife or your husband or nuzzle your partner's neck
and go to work and immerse yourself in the world of work and worry.
It's a world without angels.
It's a world without devils.
Try as they might they have no influence.
In this world all that matters is the flutter of the breeze.
The smell of rotting leaves.
The sound of a car engine.
The rough touch of your lover's beard.
In this world we own everything.
We own it.

Watch, listen, taste, smell, eat, breathe, sleep, rise, work.
These are our imperatives. They keep our lives whole.
When it's over we can talk to the angels or the devils.
It will be a brief talk.
They're always there.
They're hungry for conversation.
But then so am I.
How'd it go today?
Everything good at work?
How was your show?
Is John's company doing okay?
We can talk and talk and talk.
We can drink buckets of wine.
We can buy a new car and drive till the road ends and then walk
for miles in the woods.
Don't you just love the smell of the forest?
Or the smell of a new car?
I don't care as long as we've got something to talk about.
Something to drink to.
Someone to talk to.
So, what was your name again?
Where are you from? And your parents?
You say your father was a salesman?
That's interesting.
Keep talking, keep eating, keep drinking, keep going,
keep going, keep going.

Tonight I watched *A Prairie Home Companion*.
An Angel of Death took people to the other side.
I wept.

So, let me think about the Angel of Death for a minute.
He's far from my side right now.
I know he could come to visit at any moment.

Every time you die
or are close to dying there is someone to shepherd you.
A spirit.
An angel.
A devil.
A sprite.

They talk to you and tell you what you want
and you listen or
don't and choose or don't.
They don't care about that walk in the woods or the smell of your car.
They've never been in love.
They've never rolled over in bed with their heart heaving
after good sex.
They don't have hearts that break or tears or fun.
They don't eat tuna fish.
They don't weep at stupid movies.
They don't rail at Christmas bonuses or lousy checks.
They don't fuck around with their boss' wife.
They don't get wet in a swift storm on the way home from work.
That's our job.
So.
Do it well.
Do it every day.
Do it with relish and abandon and resignation and commitment.
Do it like there isn't anything else you'd rather do.
Do it till you die and when you do, greet your angel with a smile.
Say hello.
She'll be glad you recognize her.

Dreaming of Imps

I was very sick for a time.
I came so close to death it seemed almost like I was dead.
I spent much too much time with demons and angels.
I ate too little and slept too little and sweated through the night.
I woke each morning drenched from my dreams.

Last night there was an imp in my bed.
Well, not really an imp,
a small demon, I guess.
I woke up and must have frightened it
because it scurried off to hide in the shadows.
But I saw it.
The color of a young roach.
Twisted.
Mean.
Then it was gone.

I haven't been sick for years.
Not like before anyway.
Oh, a flu now and then, or a sore throat,
but that's been it.
Till that imp leaped up and licked my face.

There was a time such things were with me daily.
Demons and imps and shrouded ghouls
lingering by my bedside as I lay sleeping,
dreaming terrible dreams of a good life.
A life where I had a job and friends and ate food
in restaurants.
A life filled with nice clothing and cars.
People who laughed at my jokes and forgave my foibles.

The demons watched me twitch in sleep and
giggled at my travails.

Perhaps they never left.
Perhaps I'm still desperately ill.
This life is the dream I dream.
My car, my dogs, my new suits, my beloved.
All just fodder for their little jokes.
There should be an insecticide for demons and imps.
There should be some poison I could set out
for them to find and eat.
It might be unpleasant to find their swollen little bodies but
except for a day or two of stink it would be better to have them gone.

But it seems to me that there is no poison they wouldn't love.
No death they couldn't cherish.
No desire or whim that wouldn't amuse them.
Dreams and imps.

The Hardest Poem a Man Can Write

Here lies Jack
Dumb as a stick
and flat on his back.
Couldn't keep his dick in his pants.
Now there's worms in his mouth.
Thought he'd live forever.
Oops he was wrong.

Coda

The Man With the Rotten Teeth

I've been worrying a molar for two weeks
Just twirling it around and around and
waiting for it to drop.
It never does.
My gums are receding daily.
My mouth is filled with blood.
I floss clots from between my teeth in the morning.
People say, are you writing, and I say
no, it's too much like pulling teeth.
I don't care about food.
I don't care about sex.
I only want to watch TV and sleep.
Does that make me a bad person?
I like my brandy and cigar at night.
I like my New Yorker,
my quiet evenings with my dogs snoring at my side.
Does that make me wrong?
When the bile rises up in me and
I feel my heart racing and I want to scream,
I want to say, fuck you, and
I want to be the nastiest fuck on the planet,
do those thoughts make me bad?
All this anger and dullness.
What sense does it make?
How do I make sense of the blood clots,
the rotting teeth,
the rage,
the fevers, the aches,
the mouth so dry no amount of water can help?
Shall I say it's the medicine?

Should I worry that it's a disease and not the medicine?
Should I be concerned that this is who I truly am?
This mean, angry monster,
his teeth dropping from his mouth
like coarse bits of dried corn.
Is this my true self?
Oh, this a curse from God.
Oh, this is a burden to be borne.
Oh, this is the end of me and
my body of flesh and blood and bone and hair.
Oh, how I want to be back in the world,
whole and happy and
Oh, how that seems it is not to be.
Not to be.

Spring on Palisades Avenue

There is a great rush of noise outside.
Men and women tumble out of the bar
and rush against each other.
Screaming and cursing.
Spanish and English.
A young Latin guy,
shirtless, rushes up to
a black man who lays a tremendous right
on the side of the kid's head.
There are men pushing back their friends.
Women racing here and there, smoking,
furiously,
turning to their men and cursing and
there are others standing,
watching,
waiting for the next blow,
a gun maybe.
The crowd flows here and there.
Neighbors, me included, sit at their windows and watch.
Then Five-O rolls up and the crowd disperses.
Quiets.
Like a winter clipper that rolls in, the cops
chill the mob. The squad car doors open and
laughing, beefy white guys amble out.
They don't even bother much
with the angry men and women.
The firemen walk out to watch.
It's all over now.
We turn away from our windows having seen
the first fight of spring.

Better than a robin.
A harbinger.
A threat.
A closed bud close to opening.
A closed fist.
A mouth about to scream.
A gun ready to explode.
A red blossom deep in the ground
held tight by the cold and the time's
ripe for bursting.
Blood just beneath the skin held in check
by the last chill of winter.

The Truth About Lying

Let's start with the obvious.
I'm a liar.
I lie with ease and regularity.
You can tell I'm lying because my lips are moving.

I don't always tell big lies.
No one does.
Most of my lies are intended to soothe
or make someone happy.

You're beautiful.
You'll get through this.
He loves you.
This is just a phase.

Then there are the lies that are somewhere in between.
I'm in bed with someone and they look at me
and ask do you love me?
I say yes.

Their eyes light up.
They smile and nuzzle in close.
It's a lie and one I instantly regret.
But I play it out for weeks or months.

There are worse lies.
The lies you tell yourself.
I told myself I would talk to a doctor
as soon as I had coverage.

I told myself it was OK that
there were warts on my ass.

That I couldn't taste food.
That I weighed twenty pounds less than I had a week before.

I tell myself everything is fine.
I'll be all right.
I tell myself God is in the heavens and
I'm blessed.

How much of this is a lie?
How much of this is a dream?
Am I able to ever speak the truth?

God is in the heavens and
I am blessed and this is not a lie
Even if it feels like one.

Living in the Real World

A tin can rattles down the street
blown by an indifferent wind.
Lightning streaks the early spring sky.
I dream and dream I'm dreaming.
In the dream I wake and seated on my bed
are two black women.
Haitian I assume.
Both wearing blue dresses with floral decoration.
They say, don't worry.
I look just beyond them and see my lover,
her wrists swollen and red,
her face covered in red pustules.
I wake again.
Panting, my heart beating.
My dogs rise up for some unseen threat.
Their hackles all on end.
The storm passes.
The world calms.
I dream again.
A dark man leads my lover away from me.
He says, be cool man, be cool.
She's smoking a cigarette.
The smoke trails off behind her.
She doesn't even hear me.
The firemen across the street have their gear
set by their trucks.
They spent all day Sunday washing
and washing and washing their trucks.
They're waiting for an alarm,
for dark smoke to rise in the sky.
For someone to wake in a room thick with smoke,

someone to wake from a dream only to find
another terror.
Another day.

Food and Money

She says, never write about food and money.
I say, why?
I like food and money.
I say, you can't get food without money and
money is no good if you don't have food.

She says, there are rules.
I say, where?
I don't remember any rules about this.
She says, if you mix them together it's toxic.
Like a salad with hotdogs in it or pennies.
I say, hot dogs aren't toxic and
who would eat a salad with pennies?

She says, don't you remember all the meals
you ate when you were young?
All the money you spent on beef and chicken?
I say, sure I remember that.
It was like heaven.
She says, now it's gone and
you have nothing to show for it.
You've spent the money and shit out the food.

I say, yes, that's true.
I say, yes, but my belly was full.
My wallet seemed to be full forever.
The food was like a wonderful dream that
you don't want to wake up from.
She says, see you're already writing poetry.

I say, but what about my friends, the wine,
the sauces, the laughter, the silly arguments,
the waiters, the linens, the clink of glass on glass,
the happy, drunken walk home?

When I finish my little talk I wipe my mouth,
take a sip of wine,
look up and find she's gone.

Black Dogs

I sleep at night with three black dogs.
They keep me safe and let me sleep.
Johanna tells me about her cousin Albert.
He sees dogs during the day.
Not regular dogs but a single black dog.
As he drives to work he sees it at each corner.
Its paws are human hands and its eyes are stitched shut.
When we went to visit him one of my dogs woke in the night.
She barked and barked and barked at nothing.

My dogs sleep well though sometimes they twitch or bark.
In dreams they run and hunt and are afraid.
In their dreams.
Johanna is afraid for Albert.
She calls her friends, brujas and brujos, and asks what is wrong.
They tell her someone in Albert's church has put a curse on him.
They tell her how to cleanse the house.
They talk about herbs and waters and smoke and rum.
She says, Papi, I'm afraid.

One of her friends asks, has the dog crossed his path?
She says no.
The friend says, good because when it does no good can come of that.
The friend says, she sees Albert in the road.
It's a hot summer day.
Flies are lighting on his face.
A dog barks somewhere far away.
The friend says, I don't know if Albert is alive or dead.
But I do.
I know he is alive.

I know because every night three black dogs cross my path.
Every night they hunt.

Every day they lie in wait.
Hoping soon I'll be home.
Albert's dog is on the corner.
Waiting.
Hoping he'll be home soon.
Albert is hurrying.
The dog is blind and black and waiting.
Albert is on his way home.

Black dogs.
Black dog.
Cars rushing down the block.
Dogs snoring.
People praying.
Portents.
Signs.
Eyes stitched or closed in sleep.
Driving cars or lying in bed.
Black dogs black dogs black dogs.
It could be good or it could be bad.
You should light a candle for your saint.
You should pull your covers up tight under your chin.
You should say a Hail Mary.
You should reach out in the dark and comfort your dog.
She's afraid and something in the dark is hunting her.
Something huge and black and mean.
Tell her it's OK.
There is nothing there.
Sleep.
Go to sleep.
Go to sleep.

Miserly

Here is how cheap I was today.
I used Johanna's change to buy my papers.
I did splurge on iced coffee but
for lunch I had a small wonton soup and
one egg roll.
I got a free Pepsi from the company fridge.
The owner buys them for another employee but
today they were mine.
I borrowed Peter's *NY Post.*
Right now I'm thinking of how I can get
someone to buy me drinks at the bar tonight.
I have one gold dollar in my pocket.
I have one paper dollar in my wallet.
I have a soul so shriveled it looks like the rumpled bill.

What Art Is and What It Isn't

I read about Donald Barthelme and post modernism tonight
and I read about art and joy and all kinds of shit.
Art is a story.
A lost loved one.
An angry parent.
A walk down 9th Avenue on a cold February day.
Art is my anger at my stupid boss.
Art is the people walking up 33rd Street,
their umbrellas held up against the rain.
Art is the buildings you walk by.
The odd sound by Madison Square in the wind.
Art is the rough Hudson in a storm.
Art is your boss taking his insulin shot.
Art is your anger at stupid things at your job.
Misapprehensions.
Foolishness.
Windmills.
Art is a lover far away.

Art is your dogs around you in bed.
Art is the men who work every day at jobs they hate.
Art is you talking to people who barely listen
to you about their problems.
You are art.
You are a soup can.
You are a bizarre building.
You are the man letting people into Dunkin Donuts.
You are the man with a soaked and soiled jacket.
You are the damaged man floating across 8th Avenue like a ghost.
You are the sad fool in love.
Art is your joy and your loss.

Art is your job lost to budget cuts.
Art is you going to work every day
listening to men talking about writing letters
to their workers praising them with no money
behind the praise.

Art is not a toilet seat.
It's not a comic strip.
It's your glass of brandy and it's your friends who don't call.
Art is the trash on the sidewalk.
The summons for recycling.
Art is the sad poetry reading with five people.
Art is the painting that no one ever sees.
Art is the poem that no one reads.

Art is the fools in school.
Art is the teachers in the same school.
Art is the teacher that never tells his students.
I'm a poet.
Art is the only chance you have to be alive.
Art is all you have.

You could break it down into theory.
You could make fun of it.
You could say it has no purpose.
You'd be right.
You'd be walking up 33rd Street
and your umbrella bends and twists in the wind.
You're soaked in a drenching rain.
Your feet are cold.
Your lover hasn't called.
Your lunch was Chinese fried chicken wings.
Your heart is sour and cold like your feet.

Divina Is Divina

That would be art.
That would be joy.
That would be your life.

Why I Go to Work

First, because I need money.
But before I went to work
I had money, so it can't be that.
Maybe because I like the company,
but I have friends and a lover so
it's not that either.
Perhaps recognition.
No, no one cares about what I do.
No, I work because I want to work.
I want to answer phones and
write memos and complain about
my boss or the customers.
I want to read about cockroaches.
I want to go down greasy ladders
in greasy kitchens to stare at
rat shit and waterbugs skittering,
skittering,
everywhere.
I want to puzzle every day about what I'll eat.
I want to be unhappy with my choices.
I want to walk to the light rail, the PATH,
the office and I want the sun to shine at the end
of 33rd Street with NJ across the Hudson.
I want to go home with a check in my pocket.
My feet sore from walking the streets of
New York City and I want to wake up
and do it all again.
And again.
And again.

Walking with a Lunatic

I'm walking down 8th Avenue and my foot
gets a stabbing pain and I almost trip.
I say to myself, I hate my body.
And I do, I hate my body.
I hate its sagging skin and the scars inside it
that no one can see
but that I can feel.

I hate my feet with their neuropathies.
Their nerves all fucked up.
Telling me we're in pain
when we're walking on a beach.
Or else shouting, we're being stabbed
when we stepped on a tiny dog kibble.
The way they feel like hard lumps of plastic.
As though I'd changed into a monster overnight.
A monster with a hard carapace.

I hate my ears, the constant ringing,
the roar of a million crickets all day long.
All day long drowning out the cars and
lunatic arguments.
Lunatics on the corner shouting that
they can't feel their feet.
Shouting that they hate their bodies.
Turning around and around,
their dirty jackets spinning
like the jackets on whirling dancers.
Their hair whipping in the wind.
The hate palpable.
The rage divine.
The bottle in the hand spinning with the body.

They're blocking the sidewalk in front of me
so I have to slide to the left suddenly
and my fucked up body thinks it's going to the right.
I almost fall.
I almost curse my body again but I start to think
that I am my body and the ringing in the ears
is mine and the feet are joined to the heart
by the line of blood and the line
of blood runs straight to my head where I think I live
when, of course, I don't live there.
I live here in this world with its lunatics
and concrete and wooden floors and beaches
and walking and complaining is what my body and I seem to like best.

Tending Gardens

In late winter, early spring, Johanna came to Wenonah.
She was ill.
So was I.
We both were shadows of ourselves.

She ate and was given comfort.
She got care and grew strong.
My town was dull and boring.
My landlady a devout Methodist.

At times she would work with my landlady
in her garden.
It was a garden filled with flowers and herbs.
I'd look out and see the two of them bent over.

My landlady was 76 and devout.
She kept the gardens of the town and
went to church each Sunday.
Johanna was young and most decidedly not a Methodist.

One spring day Johanna walked out onto our porch.
The air was filled with the scent of lilacs and apple blossoms.
She breathed it all in and came inside.
Jack, she said, this is amazing.

It was.
Amazing.

A few years later Johanna and I went to my family's Thanksgiving.
We'd been away from South Jersey for several years.
It was a warm day.
My stepbrothers and I were in the garage watching football.

As we were talking and drinking beer
the fall leaves began to swirl in the yard.
Johanna walked out and looked at the spectacle.
The spectacle.

She said, Papi, I've never seen anything like this.
It's so beautiful.
I saw it too.
It was beautiful.

The world gave us a spectacle.
We were stunned.

But for me,
the most beautiful spectacle was an old woman
tending her garden with a gorgeous transsexual from El Salvador
in the middle of South Jersey without a word of comment.

Without a word of comment.

CAVANKERRY'S MISSION

Through publishing and programming, CavanKerry Press connects communities of writers with communities of readers. We publish poetry that reaches from the page to include the reader, by the finest new and established contemporary writers. Our programming brings our books and our poets to people where they live, cultivating new audiences and nourishing established ones.

OTHER BOOKS IN
THE NOTABLE VOICES SERIES